T0077896

The BEST GREEN BAY FOOTBALL

PET NAMES

DR. JON KESTER

authorHOUSE

AuthorHouse™
1663 Liberty Drive
Bloomington, IN 47403
www.authorhouse.com
Phone: 833-262-8899

Published by AuthorHouse 06/09/2022

ISBN: 978-1-6655-6213-3 (sc)
ISBN: 978-1-6655-6212-6 (e)

Library of Congress Control Number: 2022911040

Dedication

This book is dedicated to my very special kitten, Kit-Kat. He loved to watch Don Majikowski and Tim Harris play in the late 1980s and early 1990s.

Contents

Importance of choosing a pet's name

Are you overwhelmed at the thought of choosing a name for your newfound family member? Picking the perfect name for your new pet can be stressful, but this book is here to help. Rather than giving you a list of the most trendy names to choose from, I thought it would it would be helpful to list inspirational Green Bay Packers names along with the important contributions each player made to the Green and Gold. So, whether you are looking for a unique name or one that matches your pet's personality, I hope the Green Bay Packers can help you choose the perfect pet name.

WHY SHOULD I NAME MY PET AFTER A PACKER?

The big question that comes up is why I should name my pet after a Green Bay Packer player and not after my math teacher in 6th grade or my favorite food. Well the four main reasons are:

1) The Packer are champions
2) The Packers are Hall of Famer
3) The Packers are loyal
4) The Packers are a class act

Champions

The Green Bay Packers have won more championships (13) than any other team in National Football League history.

They won their first three by league standing (1929, 1930 and 1931), and 10 since the NFL's playoff system was established in 1933,1936, 1939, 1944, 1961, 1962, 1965, 1966, 1967, 1996 and 2010). Green Bay also is the only NFL team to win three straight titles, having done it twice (1929-30-31 and 1965-66-67). (https://www.packers.com/history/championship-seasons)

In addition, the Packers won the first two Super Bowls (over Kansas City in 1966, 35-10, and over Oakland in 1967, 33-14), as well as two more recently (over New England in 1996, 35-21, and over Pittsburgh in 2010, 31-25). (https://www.packers.com/history/championship-seasons)

Every pet owner should want their animal to be a champion. Giving your pet a sweet sounding Packer name could be the first step.

Hall of Famers

Over the 100 year history of the NFL 28 players have entered the Pro Football Hall of Fame as Green Bay Packers. Players like Don Hutson, Bart Starr, Brett Favre and Reggie White have come to define what it means to play for the Packers. According to C. David Baker, the President of the Pro Football hall of fame. "A Hall of Famer is someone who has given all they had on and off the field, had a high peak in their career, and was elite at his position."

All pet owners should want a Hall of Famer fur baby, an animal who will grow up to give all to make their new owner happy.

Loyalty to their team

No group of fans is as loyal to their team as the Cheese heads that fill Lambeau Field for everything from practices to playoff games. The Frozen Tundra has been sold out for every game since 1960. According to the Green Bay ticket office, the season-ticket waiting list now has 86,000 names on it, and management estimates a turnover of 90 tickets each year. If you put your name on the list now, you can expect to be attending home games in the year 2067. Despite the nearly 1,000-year waiting list, new names are added to it every season. Every new pet owner deserves to have pet around them who are loving and loyal; this could be part of your pet's future if you pick an amazing Packer name for them.

Being a Class Act:

For the Green Bay Packers, winning football games the "right way" has always been important. The organization has always maintained a standard for class and dignity that applies to management, coaches, players and everyone else involved with the franchise. The Packer has long been a reflection of the friendly, blue-collar people that populate Wisconsin.

A winning tradition was established early on in Green Bay, and this has molded the franchise into what it is today. The people involved with the organization have changed, but certain standards have remained. Everyone involved with the franchise is expected to maintain a certain level of esteem for their teammates and the organization. Things in Green Bay are always done in a way that shows respect for the game, the team and the history of the two. Every pet owner wants a pet whose actions they can be proud of.

It should be every pet owners dream to have a new animal that is a Champion in life with a Hall of fame personality that is loyal and a class act. So have fun with this book and good luck finding an amazing pet name for your little furry cheese head.

Names from the early years of the packers (1919-1956)

In 1919 Curly Lambeau and George Calhoun organized a group of men in Green Bay, Wisconsin into a football team that soon became the best team in the Midwest. Lambeau, a former high school football star, who went on to play college ball at Notre Dame was currently a shipping clerk for the Indian Packing Company when he convinced his employer to donate money for the uniforms and, in the process, lent the nickname "Packers" to the team. With Lambeau serving as head coach and playing halfback, in 1921 the Packers entered the recently formed American Professional Football Association, which a year later would become the NFL.

In the early years the Packers struggled with financial problems to the point of having to forfeit an entire season in 1922. The following year the team became a publicly owned nonprofit corporation supported by the people of Wisconsin and has remained so ever since.

Despite their rough financial start, the Packers won three consecutive championships from 1929 to 1931, with lineups that were laden with future Hall of Famers, including tackle Cal Hubbard, guard Mike Michalske, and halfback John ("Blood") McNally. In 1935 the team added Don Hutson, who proceeded to redefine the wide receiver position and helped the Packers win championships in 1936, 1939, and 1944. Lambeau—who stopped playing for the team in 1929—stepped away from head coaching duties in 1949, and the team struggled for wins throughout the next decade: the Packers posted a losing record seven times between 1950 and 1958. The early years in the Packers history have some legendary names for your new pet.

Best Pet names from the early years:

Bucket's – is the nickname of Charles "Buckets" Goldenberg. Bucket's was a hall of fame caliber guard for the Packers from

1933 to 1945. He is a member of the 1930s all decade team and went to college at the University of Wisconsin- Madison.

Buckets would be an ok pet name for a Basset hound or Beagle or maybe a basketball playing cat. At first the name sound lame but it does kind of grow on you, so give it a try.

Buford - is the first name of Buford " baby" ray. Buford played tackle for the Packers from 1938 to 1948. He is a member of the 1940s all decade team and 4 time all pro.

Buford is an awesome name for a big ole pet that doesn't move around much. A pet named Buford is not going to be one that is running around chasing a Frisbee but could be a loyal pet that likes to takes naps with you and lay around all day.

Canadeo - is the last name of Legendary Packer running back Tony Canadeo. Canadeo was the most talented halfback for the Packers from 1941-1952. In 1949 Tony became the third player in NFL history to rush for 1,000 or more yards in a season. He retired as the Packers' all-time rushing yards leader. Canadeo's jersey number "3" was retired by the Packers immediately following his retirement as a player. He was inducted into the Pro Football Hall of Fame and Wisconsin Athletic Hall of Fame and the Green Bay Packers Hall of Fame.

Canadeo would be a great name for an athletic breed of dog like a Labrador or maybe even a bird like a Cockatoo a pet named after Tony Canadeo needs to be an impressive runner / flyer with a hall of fame personality.

Carmichael – is the last name of Al Carmichael who was a half back and kicks returner for the Packers from 1953 to 1958. According to Lee Remmel, Packer historian,Carmichael was known as one of the fastest players during the 1950's and once had 106 yard kick return. Which is still in the record books as the third longest in NFL history.

Carmichael would be an amazing name for fluffy cat like a Persian or maybe a small breed of dog like a Corgi or a York Terrier. If you name your pet after Al Carmichael it needs to be a dignified breed.

Clarke- is the first name of Clark Hinkle. The Packer hall of fame claims Hinkle was widely regarded by teammates and opponents alike as one of the toughest, most talented and dedicated players of the Iron Man Era, which covered the first three decades of pro football. Clark Hinkle played running back for the packers from 1932 to 1941 and was inducted into the pro football hall of fame in 1964.

Clarke could be a great universal name for any pet but to make it super awesome you as a pet owner would need to make its full name Clarke Hinkle. The full name like with my kiddos would only come out when your pet is misbehaving. Just remember that if you name your pet after this Packer legend they could become tough as nails and well respected by all other pets in the neighborhood.

Hutson – is the last name of one of the all-time NFL and packer great Don Hutson. Don Hutson played for the packers from 1935-1945 and was a receiver who redefined the position; he is credited with creating many of the modern pass routes used in the NFL to. Hutson held almost all major receiving records at the time of his retirement, including career receptions, yards, and touchdowns. Even some 75 years later he still holds over 10 NFL records. Don Hutson was a three time NFL Champion, a two time NFL MVP, member of the NFL 75th anniversary team and both a member of the NFL and Green Bay Packers hall of fame.

Hudson would be a lofty name for a golden retriever since he was a golden receiver it just makes sense or for a bad dad joke. If you decide to name your pet after Don Hutson they could be an All –Time great record setting pet. Seriously this would be an awesome name for any true Packers fan pet. So use this name!

Isbell – is the last name of Cecil Isbell, who was a star half back for the Packers from 1938 to 1942. Isbell was one of the best players during the late 1930s being named an All Pro three times. He was also elected to the Packers hall of fame in 1972

Isbell would be a grand name for a cat breed like Bombay or most birds. If you decide to name your pet after Cecil Isbell they could have a super star life.

Kiesling – is the last name of Walt Kiesling, who was one of the best players in the 1920's. Kiesling played only two years for the Packers in 1935 and 1936 but had a big impact on the team's training since he was known for being in tip top shape year round. After his playing career Walt coached for 25 years.

Kiesling would be a good name for a fish or hamster. Why I really don't know I just don't think it rolls off the tongue very well and a new pet owner would not want to have yell it over and over for their dog or cat to come.

Lambeau – is the Last name of Earl Curly Lambeau. Just in case you are a Packer fan who lives under a rock here is who Curly Lambeau is: According to the Packer hall of fame "Lambeau was the guiding force behind the creation and improbable survival of the small-town Packers in big league football. He also was the team's first star and one of the most successful coaches in NFL history." Not only did Lambeau co-found the packers he also won 6 NFL Championships. Plus not to mention the Packers stadium is named after him.

Lambeau would be an impressive name for any and all pets. If you name your pet after Curly Lambeau they could be iconic and maybe a have giant statue made of them or maybe a stadium named after them. Bottom line this is a go-to name for any Packer fan pet lover. Please name your pet Lambeau.

Lavvie – is the nickname to LaVern "Lavvie" Dilweg who played End for The Packers from 1927 to 1934. He was a three time NFL champion and a member of the 1920s NFL All – Decade team. Dilweg is also in the Green Bay Packer Hall of fame and later in life even represented Wisconsin in the U.S House of Representatives.

Lavvie would be an awesome dog's name I'm thinking a Lab or maybe a tabby cat. A pet named after Lavvie Dilweg could be a loyal champion.

Laws – is the last name of Joe Laws, who played halfback and defensive back for the Packers from 1934 to 1945. Law holds the record for intercepting 3 passes in a title game and was known for being one of the best pass defenders of the 1940's.

Laws would be a great name for any pet with paws. "Laws with paws" has a nice ring to it. I specifically could also see a German Shepheard who could have a day job as a police dog with this name.

Lewellen – is the last name of Verne Lewellen, who was a back and punter for the packers from 1924-1932. The Packers hall of fame has him down as one of the greatest all-around backs in the NFL's first three decades; Lewellen also was widely regarded as one of the NFL's greatest punters. He was a 3 time all pro player and is also a Packer hall of Famer.

Lewellen would be a noble name for any pet. Again this name doesn't roll off the tongue so maybe stay away from a pet that gets its name called a lot. Verne Lewellen played a great role in the history of Packers and this name should not be over looked.

McNally – is the last name of john "Blood" McNally one of the most iconic and talented player to ever put on a packer uniform. He played running back from 1929 to 1936. According to the Packer Hall of fame he was born John Victor McNally but adopted the alias Johnny Blood while playing sandlot football and turned it into one of the most magical names in sports. It also was a fitting name for one of the game's most colorful and eccentric players. Most important, Blood was pro football's first big playmaker. McNally played on their first four NFL championship teams and was known for his ability to score from anywhere on the field at any time. He was elected into the NFL hall of fame is 1963.

McNally could be a great name for a bloodhound it could be named Johnny "bloodhound" McNally. McNally would also be a great name for an Irish Setters or a Manx cat. A pet with this name could grow up to be an eccentric legend whose name will echo throughout history.

Michalske - is the last name of NFL great Mike Michalske. According to the Packer Hall of Fame Michalske is "Widely regarded as one of the greatest guards in the first 30 years of the NFL." Michalske was a member of the 1920's All-Decade team and was elected into the Pro football hall of fame in 1964.

Michalske was an amazing player but not so good of a pet name. Maybe a fish or a turtles could fit well with this name. Again, something you don't have to say on a daily basis due to the fact the name is just hard to pronounce and doesn't role off the tongue well.

Remmel - is the last name of Lee Remmel who was a green bay sports writer and then later Green Bay Packers public relations director and team historian. Remmel was an eyewitness to Packers history like few others. He spent nearly three decades writing about them for the Green Bay Press-Gazette. He then spent more than three decades working for the team in public relations and as team historian. As a sportswriter, Remmel chronicled every coach from Curly Lambeau to Dan Devine

Remmel would be an honorable name for a Rottweiler or a Russian tabby cat. Remmel also sounds like a good fit for a larger bird that deserves a lot of respect.

Rose- is the last name of Al Rose. Al was an end for the Packers from 1932 to 1936. He was best known for being a college star from the University of Texas and for having some of the best hands in the NFL.

Rose is a great name for any pet. However instead of telling people your pet is named after a wussy flower, you can say she was named after Al Rose who was a rough and tumble Packer player.

Tiny - is the nickname of Paul "tiny" Engebretsen. Tiny was an offensive lineman for the pack from 1934 to 1941. He was a member of 3 NFL championship teams. In 1978, Engebretsen was elected into the Packers hall of fame.

Tiny is a good ironic name for a large pet like a Mastiff or St. Bernard. I personally always liked the name Tiny for a turtle. Just make sure you tell all your friends that your pet was named after an old school Packer Paul "tiny" Engebretsen.

Tobin – is the first name of Tobin Rote. He played Quart back for the Packers from 1950 to 1956. He was a shining star on some of the Packers worse teams in the history of the organization. Tobin lead the NFL in touch downs twice and was one of the best rushing quarterbacks in history, currently ranked 7th all time.

Tobin would be a nice pet name for s turtle or a tabby cat. A pet named after Tobin Rote could be a bright spot when everything else around them is dark.

Zatkoff – is the last name of Roger Zatkoff. Roger played for the packers from 1953 to 1956. During that time he was a standout linebacker who went to the Pro Bowl in 1954, 1955, 1956. The University of Michigan give an Award to the team's best Linebacker each year named after Zatkoff.

Zatkoff was a legendary college player and a stand out packer however very few pets will fit this powerful name. I could not find any Cat, Dog or reptile breed that starts with a Z to do some name alliteration with so good luck with this one.

Names from the Lombardi era

The team's most successful period was in the 1960s, under the legendary coach Vince Lombardi, who had been hired in 1959. Lombardi's Packer teams in the '60s were stocked with talent, boasting future Hall of Fame players on offense and defense: quarterback Bart Starr, fullback Jim Taylor, halfback Paul Hornung, tackle Forrest Gregg, linebacker Ray Nitschke, end Willie Davis, tackle Henry Jordan, cornerback Herb Adderley, and safety Willie Wood. They won championships in 1961 and 1962 and followed with three straight championships starting in the 1965–66 season. On January 15, 1967, in the inaugural Super Bowl, the Packers defeated the Kansas City Chiefs 35–10. They successfully defended their Super Bowl title the following year against the Oakland Raiders, 33–14. The Lombardi era is loaded with amazing football players who have impressive names that live on in history. This is a great era to find an awesome pet name!!

Best Pet names in the Lombardi era

Adderley- is the last name of Herb Adderley. Herb was an all-decade cornerback who played on 6 national championship teams. Herb Adderley was also a great return guy on special teams and was known for his lightning fast speed.

Adderley would be a great bird name or maybe a fast running dog breed like a grey hound or a Dalmatian. A pet named after this Hall of Fame great could be a true champion and be very swift.

Aldridge- is the last name of Lionel Aldridge. Lionel was a defensive end for the Packers from 1963 to 1971. He was a three time NFL Champion and a member of the Green Bay Packers Hall of Fame.

Aldridge would be a nice name for a cat maybe a Persian also

I can also see a smaller dog with a lot of class like a Corgi being named after this Packer legend.

Bart – is the first name of all-time great Green bay packer, Bart Starr. Starr is one of only 6 Packers in the last 100 years to have his number retired. Bart Starr also was the field general for 5 NFL championship teams. This man is an iconic Packer and should be one of the first names that come up when naming your new pet.

Bart would be an amazing name for any dog. I envision a boy going to the lake fishing with his black lab named Bart A pet named after Bart Starr will be an all-time great loyal friend.

Bobby Dillon – is the full name of one of the greatest and under-rated Packer players of all time. Dillion is the Packers all-time leader in interceptions and was a 4 time all pro player. He did all of this with just one working eye.

Bobby Dillon could be a great name for a fish, turtle, snake, or maybe most types of birds. The best part of using this name is that if you ever give up on the Packers you can shorten your pets name to Bob Dillion and say he was named after the legendary folk singer.

Boyd – is the first name of Boyd Dowler. He was an all-star wide receiver and punter from 1959 to 1969. Boyd was named rookie of the year in 1959. He also was a member of the 1960s all decade team and was a 5 time NFL champion.

Boyd would be a good name for a Burmese cat or a Bull dog or maybe a pet bear. A pet named after Boyd Dowler would be a true winner for its new owner.

Chandler – is the last name of Don Chandler. Chandler was the Packers kicker and punter from 1965 to 1967. He was one of the best kickers of the 1960s and was named to the all-decade team. Don Chandler was also voted into the Packers hall of fame in 1975.

Chandler would be a wonderful name for both dogs and cats along with most birds and some fish. A pet named after Chandler could be a great kicker with a champion leg. Chandler is also a good compromise name for you and your wife. She could tell people your pet is named after some wussy TV character and you can tell your friends the truth he was named after a legendary Packer kicker.

Cochran – is the last name of long time Packers coach and scout John "Red" Cochran. Cochran worked for the Packers for 42 years which is one of the longest tenures of anyone in football operations over the storied life of the franchise.

Red was a great coach and football man but only a few pets should bear his name. My first thought would be bird like a cockatoo, cockatiel or even a little canary.

Currie – is the last name of Dan Currie, who was a linebacker for the Packers from 1958 to 1964. Dan is a two time world champion and was known as one of the hardest hitting defensive players in the 1960s era.

Currie would be a great name for a kitten mores specifically a Siamese or Calico.

Forrest – is the First name of Legendary tackles Forrest Gregg. Gregg was a key player on the Packers dynasty of head coach Vince Lombardi that won five NFL championships and the first two Super Bowls in the 1960s. He played mostly at right tackle, but also filled in at guard. Gregg earned an "iron-man" tag by playing in a then-league record 188 consecutive games in sixteen seasons, from 1956 until 1971.

Forrest would be a great dog name specifically for a Siberian husky or Dogue de Bordeaux. If your new pet is named Forrest they could end up being very trustworthy and dependable.

Hanner- is the last name of Dave Hanner. This gentleman, dedicated 42 years of his life to the Green Bay Packers. Hanner played defense tackle from 1952 to 1964. After the 1964 season he became a coach and then later on a scout for the Packers. Very few men have been as loyal to the Packers as Dave. Hanner.

Hanner would be a good name for a Newfoundland, St. Bernard or pretty much any large dog . If you name your new pet is named after Dave Hanner they could be one of the devoted packer fans ever. Just be sure to stay away from Hanner's nick name when naming your pet unless it's fat and likes to eat. He was commonly known as "Hawg" Hanner.

Hornung- is the last name of Green Bay Packers "golden boy", Paul Hornung. Paul was one of the greatest running backs of all time, having won the Heisman trophy in college for being the best college player which was followed up by an MVP in 1961 while playing on one of the greatest Packer teams of all time.

Hornung was one of the most impressive players to ever put on the green and gold, however only a few pets would fit this famous name. I would suggest a dog like a hound dog or a havapoo.

Gillingham - is the last name of Gale Gillingham, who played for the Packers from 1966 to 1976. During his playing time Gillingham was named all-pro 6 times and was a member of two NFL championship teams. Gale Gillingham was one of the strongest Packers ever and was known for spending hours in the weight room which helped contribute to his ten years of dominance.

Gillingham would be a great name for a fish (since they have gills) or maybe a dog like a Great Dane or German Shepard.

Jeter - is the last name of Bob Jeter. Jeter was a hard hitting corner back who was part of three of Lombardi's Championship teams. He was also a two time pro bowler and is in the Green Bay Packers hall of fame.

Jeter would be a good name for an athletic pet with lots of speed. I could picture a cat like the Egyptian Mau or Bengal or a dog like a Saluki. A pet named after Bob Jeter could be a great pass defender or maybe a fan of the Yankees.

Jordan – is the last name of hall of famer Henry Jordan. Jordan was a stout defensive tackle for ten years. During this time Henry Jordan was a 7 times all-pro and 5 time world champion.

Jordan would be a great name for any pet and if you're a fan of the Packers and a certain all-time great Basketball player you get the best of both worlds with this name.

Kramer – is the last name of Jerry Kramer, who played from 1958 to 1968 for the Green Bay Packers. Kramer is one of the most popular Packer players of all-time. He was a 5 time NFL Champion and a member of the 1960s all-decade team. Jerry Kramer is also known for his best-selling book called "Instant Replay" and finally was voted into the Pro Football hall of fame in 2018.

Kramer is an iconic Packer name and works again for most pets. I think it sounds awesome to say look there is Kramer the cat.

Max McGee - is the full name of the Lombardi eras best wide receiver. He is a five time NFL champion and a member of the Green Bay Packers hall of fame. Max McGee is also famous for being a celebrity restaurateur, having co-founded the restaurant Chi-Chi's.

Max McGee is a nice name for most dogs specifically, a

German Shepard or larger dog. I do not see this as a good bird or fish name but you never know.

Mercein – is the last name of Chuck Mercein. Chuck played for the Packers from 1967-to 1969. Mercein was born and raised in the Milwaukee, Wisconsin area. He was also well known for his brain as well as his brawn as he graduated college from Yale.

Mercein would be a noble name for a pet from France like a Berger Picard, Papillon,or a Barbet for dog breads or Chartreux for cats.

Nitschke- is the last name of all-time great Packer Ray Nitschke. Ray was one of the greatest linebackers in NFL history and was known for his toughness. Nitschke is one of only 6 players in Packer history to have his number retired.

Nitschke is not a name for just any pet. A pet named after Ray Nitschke will be one bad ass S.O.B. and as their new owner you better be ready!

Ringo – is the Last name of Jim Ringo, who played center for the Packers from 1953 to 1963. Ringo was a 10 time Pro Bowl center and two time NFL championship. Jim Ringo was a member of the 1960's All Decade team and was voted into the Pro football hall of fame in 1981.

Ringo is a great pet name for all dogs and some cats. The cat breeds would be ocicat, toyger or European shorthair. It would also be great for an exotic pet like a ring tailed lemur.

Starr- is the last name of Bart Starr. Yes, His first name was already mentioned but this man is so nice his name is on the list twice.

Starr would be an absolute amazing name for all pets. A pet named after Bart Starr would truly be a shining part of your life.

Taylor – is the last name of packer great Jim Taylor . Mr. Taylor was a hard running fullback from 1958 to 1966. During his time in Green bay he was named NFL MVP in 1962 and was a member of 4 championship teams. According to most defensive players from the 1960s Jim Taylor was the hardest man in football to tackle.

Taylor would be a great baby name for most pets I could picture dog breeds such as golden retriever, American pit bull terrier or a border collie. Cat breeds such as Persians, Bombay's would do well with this name. Remember to remind people your pet is NOT named after an annoying blonde pop singer but an amazing football player.

Thurston – is the last name of Fred "Fuzzy" Thurston. Fuzzy was a member of the legendary Packers offensive line from the 1960's. Thurston is a home grown Wisconsin guy, growing up in Altoona and is one of only a handful of NFL players who was a member of 6 championship teams.

Thurston is a hall of fame pet name for the certain large strong pet like a American bull dog, shar pei, or St Bernard.

Vince- is the first name of Vince Lombardi. Lombardi is the Greatest coach in NFL history, Period. No coach in National Football League history achieved more success in less time than Lombardi did during his nine seasons in Green Bay. He won five NFL championships, including Super Bowls I and II, and compiled a remarkable 89-29-4 regular-season record. Lombardi was also one of the greatest leaders in the history of America.

Vince is an all-time great green bay Packer's pet name. The only reason you do not name your new pet Vince is because you already have three pet's named Vince and your house is getting kind of confusing with so many Vince's running around.

Zeke - is the first name of Zeke Bratkowski, who was the backup quarterback in Green Bay from 1963 to 1968. Bratkowski later became a coach for the Packers and is a member of the National Polish sports Hall of fame.

Zeke was a loyal Packer Backer for many years and would be a solid pet name for a turtle, fish and some snakes. It would also be a good name for a laid back cat or a medium sized dog that is always by your side.

Names from the dark ages
aka 1970's and 80s

For about a quarter-century after Lombardi's departure, the Packers had relatively little on-field success. In the 22 seasons from 1968 to 1989, they had only five seasons with a winning record, one being the shortened 1982 strike season. They appeared in the playoffs twice, with a 1–2 record. The period saw five different head coaches – Phil Bengtson, Dan Devine, Bart Starr, Forrest Gregg, and Lindy Infante – two of whom, Starr and Gregg, were Lombardi's era stars, while Bengtson was a former Packer coach. Each led the Packers to a worse record than his predecessor. Poor personnel decisions were rife, notoriously the 1974 trade by acting general manager Dan Devine which sent five 1975 or 1976 draft picks (two first-rounders, two second-rounders and a third) to the Los Angeles Rams for aging quarterback John Hadl, who would spend only 1½ seasons in Green Bay.[19] Another came in the 1989 NFL Draft, when offensive lineman Tony Mandarich was taken with the second overall pick ahead of Barry Sanders, Deion Sanders, and Derrick Thomas. Though rated highly by nearly every professional scout at the time, Mandarich's performance failed to meet expectations, earning him ESPN's ranking as the third "biggest sports flop" in the last 25 years.

Though the teams during this era of Packer history sucked there were some outstanding names to choose from for your new pet. Here is a comprehensive list to choose from:

The best names from the 1970s and 1980s

Brockington – is the last name of John Brockington. John was a star running back for the Packers in the 1970s. He was named to 3 pro bowls and was the rookie of the year in 1971. John Brockington was known for his strength and powerful running style which would punish anyone who tried to tackle him.

Brockington would be a great name for a tough pet a Rottweiler or Doberman. If you name your pet after John Brockington no one in their "right mind" would mess with you or your pet.

Buchanon – is the last name of Willie Buchanon, who was a cornerback for the Packers from 1972 to 1978. During his Packer career he was a two time pro bowl player and was the defense rookie of the year.

Buchanon would be an awesome name for a pet dog, cat or fish. The breads of dogs such as beagles and Bolognese would be honored to be named after this Packer great.

Carr- is the last name of Green Bay Packer linebacker Fred Carr. Fred was one of the best defensive players in the 1970s. In fact he was a 3 time pro bowler and a Green Bay Packer hall of famer.

Carr would be a great for your special feline friend. Carr the cat sounds amazing!

Coffman – is the last name of one of Green Bay's greatest tight end, Paul Coffman. Paul is a member of the Green Bay Packers hall of fame and was known of having the best combination of catching and blocking ability in the NFL during the 1980s.

Coffman would be a wonderful name for a turtle or some types of freshwater fish. Also Coffman the cat has a divine ring to it, so consider it for your feline friend.

Dickey- is the last name of the beloved Packer quarterback Lynn Dickey. Lynn is a Packer Hall of Famer and was one of the Best passers in the 1980s.

Dickey could be a nice name for a dog. However, be careful when you ask the neighbors if they saw your "little Dickey". (Yes, I still have the mentality of a middle school student)

Dilweg – is the last name of former Packer Quarterback Anthony Dilweg. Anthony was a good college quarterback and was a back-up in Green Bay for 3 year.

Dilweg would be a nice name for a Guinee pig or a dog with big floppy ears. I could also see a cat with a goofy personality name Dilweg as well.

Ellis- is the last name of Green Bay Packer Gerry Ellis. Gerry was a hardtop tackle running back for the pack from 1980 to 1986. Ellis is also a member of the Green Bay Packers hall of fame.

Ellis would be a nice name for a pet iguana. Ellis also could work for a beagle or smaller but athletic breed of dog.

Harris- is the last name of Green Bay Packers defensive stud Tim Harris. Harris was a Packer linebacker from 1986- to 1990, he was a two time pro-bowler and in 1989 was defensive player of the year having recorded 19.5 sacks.

Harris would be a great pet name for a hamster or would work with a large breed of dog again like a boxer or bull terrier. I could also see a charming cat with this name as well.

John Jefferson – is the full name of one of Green Bay's most dynamic wide receivers in the 1980s. John was a four time pro bowler and a member of a number of different football hall of fames.

John Jefferson would be an amazing pet name for a Persian cat or maybe a bird like a cockatoo. This name is meant for a pet of great nobility.

MacArthur – is the first name of MacArthur Lane, who played for the Packers from 1972 to 1974. Lane was a scoring machine and once scored 11 touchdowns in one season. He was also known for his powerful running and was nicknamed the truck.

MacArthur would be a good pet name for a Macaw. It also works for most large breeds of dogs or many types of cats as well. There is just something about this name that has a nice ring to it.

Majkowski- is the last name of Don Majkowski. Don was a Packer from 1987 to 1992 and was a pro-bowler and passing leader during that time. Majkowski was the quarterback who got injured and started the Brett Favre era.

Majkowski is a name that just does not roll of the tongue and should be avoided unless you live in Pulaski, or Stevens Point Wisconsin, where a large amount of Polish pets live. In these communities the name Majkowski is very common and most families have at least one or two pets named after the Polish prince of football .

Mandarich – is the last name of Packers first round draft pick bust Tony Mandarich. Referred to as "the best offensive line prospect ever",[Mandarich was highly touted during his collegiate career at Michigan State, leading to his high selection in the 1989 draft by the Packers. However, Mandarich was unable to live up to expectations and was released following four seasons with the team

Mandarich is a named maybe for a turtle or a dog that didn't live up to its expectations. If you are looking for a unique name for a pet that does have Packer history then go with Mandarich but personally I would go with Favre or Hutson or Reggie or anything else.

McCarren -is the last name of Packer Great and long-time radio announcer Larry McCarren. Larry was a pro bowl center who was known as the " rock" for his ability to play in 162 consecutive games.

McCarren would be a decent pet name a fish or Guinee pig. It again is name that doesn't roll of the tongue for a pet you call a lot like a dog but that is just my humble opinion.

Lofton- is the last name of James Lofton. James played wide receiver for the Packers from 1978 to 1986 and was an 8 time pro bowler. Lofton was one of the only players to catch a touchdown pass in the 1970s, 1980s, 1990's and is a member of both the Green Bay Packers and Pro football hall of fame.

Lofton would be a great name for any pet bird that loves to soar. I would also recommend this name for any dog that loves to play fetch as well. Overall, Lofton is a great pet name.

Odom- is the last name of Steve Odom, who was a wide receiver and kick returner for the Packers from 1974 to 1979. Odom was one of the best punt returners in the game and holds the Packers record for returning a punt 95 yards for a touchdown against the bears in 1974.

Odom would be a nice name for most dogs and cats. The name is nice, short and easy for owners to call out and for pets to understand.

Stenerud- is the last name of Packers kicker Jan Stenerud. Jan is a hall of fame kicker who played for the Packers from 1980 to 1983. He was also named to the NFL 75th anniversary team. Jan Stenerud is one of the greatest special team's players in the history of the NFL.

Stenerud would be a great name a very special pet like a fish, hamster, bird and some reptiles. Unlike the name above it, this name is hard to say and would be challenging to have to yell or say a lot. With that being said the man with this name was one heck of a kicker!

Woodfield- is the last name of Randall Woodfield. He was a wide receiver drafted in the 17th round in 1974. ***All you have to do is google the name Randall Woodfield and you will know why no pet EVER should have this name. ***

Brett Favre era names

In 1992 the Packers traded for a little known quarterback named Brett Favre, who would become the key piece in the team's renaissance in the 1990s up until the mid-2000. Beginning in 1993, Green Bay qualified for the postseason in six straight years, including two NFC championships and subsequent trips to the Super Bowl. The team's third Super Bowl appearance, in 1997, was a success: they defeated the New England Patriots 35–21. However, they did not repeat their win the following year against the Denver Broncos. During this tine Brett Favre was the best player in the NFL becoming the only player to win three straight MVP awards but the team remained a play-off contender into the 21st century. Favre acrimoniously left the Packers in 2008, and the Packers' offense was given over to young star quarterback Aaron Rodgers.

The Favre era has some of the best pet names in all of Packer history. Look though the following list a pick a good one!

The top baby names from the Favre era.

Barnett – is the last name of long time Packer linebacker Nick Barnett. Nick was a first round pick in 2003 and was both a Super Bowl Champion and all pro during his Packer career.

Barnett would be a good name for a dog. Barnett the beagle has an amazing ring to it. The name could also be used for a sleek cat as well.

Bennett- is the last name of Edgar Bennett. Edgar was one of the premier running backs for the Packers in the 1990s. In fact he was the first Packer to rush for 1,000 yards in a generation. Edgar Bennett was part of the great super bowl 31 team and is a member of the Green Bay Packers Hall of Fame.

Bennett is a great name for any loyal pet and could be used again with alliteration, which I love to use so much throughout this book. Examples would be Bennett the Burmese python.

Brett Favre – is the full name of one Packers all-time greats. Favre was one of the people responsible for turning around the Packer organization from 20 plush years of being a laughing stock of the NFL.

Brett holds many NFL records, including most career pass attempts and most consecutive starts by a player. At the time of his retirement, he was the NFL's all-time leader in passing yards, passing touchdowns and quarterback wins; all three records have since been broken.

Brett Favre again is one of those names that is Packer royalty and should be used with any and all pets.

Brooks- is the last name of Robert Brooks. Robert Brooks was one of the star receivers of the 1990's for the Packers. Brooks is known for two major events, one being having the longest touchdown in Packers history, the second is making the Lambeau leap (which Leroy butler invented) popular with his rap song "Jump in the Stands".

Brooks would be a nice name for a smaller pet like a fish or hamster or smaller dog that is jumpy and athletic.

Bubba- is the nick name of tight end, Daniel BUBBA Franks. Bubba was a 3 time pro bowler and was one of Brett Favre's favorite red zone targets in the early 2000s.

Bubba would be an amazing name for a big ol dog or cat. This name is pretty universal for most animals in fact I once had a turtle name Bubba.

Butler- is the last name of Leroy Butler. Leroy was one of the best Safeties during the 1990s. He was a four time all-pro player and the first player in NFL history to record 20 sacks and 20 interceptions. Butler was also the first Packer to Jump in the stands after Reggie White recovered a fumble and flipped it to him where he went into the end zone.

Butler would be an awesome name for most dogs and some birds maybe even a fish. Why? I really don't know but Butler a hall of fame player and pet name.

Clifton – is the last name of long time offensive tackle, Chad Clifton. Chad established a reputation as one of the NFL's best and unheralded blindside blockers for Brett Favre. He Was a two time pro-bowler and a Packer hall of famer.

Clifton would be a nice name for a big red dog or any K-9 friend in general. Clifton is a name that also works well most cats as well.

Desmond – is the first name of Packer special teams star Desmond Howard. Desmond was a college superstar winning the Heisman trophy before coming to the Packers. While on the Packers he was the super bowl 31 MVP and an all-pro player.

Desmond would be an awesome name for most pets. It is just one of those names that feels comfortable to say and seems that any pet named after Desmond would be very much loved.

Detmer- is the last name of quarterback Ty Detmer. Ty was Brett Favre's back up from 1992-1995. He is most famous for winning the Heisman trophy in 1990.

Wow !!! this era has tons of good names that start with "D" and that all sound great for dogs. Detmer would be a great name for one specific breed, a Doberman.

Dorsey- is the first name of Packers running back, Dorsey Levens. Dorsey was a great combination of a power rusher along with a great pair of receiving hands. He was a pro bowler in 1997 and is also a member of the Green Bay Packer hall of fame.

Dorsey would be a fine name for a pet horsey or maybe a pet dolphin. This name sounds good with most fish and some birds as well.

Favre- is the last name of all-time great Brett Favre. His name is on this list twice because he was such a great Packer and because there are a ton of pets all over Wisconsin with this name. Remember that Favre is one if not the best Packer Pet name.

Ferguson – is the last name of wide receiver, Robert Ferguson. Robert was a second round pick of the Packers in 2001 and was one of Brett Favre's favorite targets for five years.

Ferguson would be a nice name for a cat. Just image telling your friends there goes Ferguson the feline.

Harlan- is the last name of former Green Bay Packers president, Bob Harlan. During Harlan's 19 years as head of the organization, the Packers won a Super Bowl and became one of the NFL's exemplary franchises. He also put the franchise on firm financial footing for years to come as the driving force behind the redevelopment of Lambeau Field as a year-round destination.

Harlan would make a great name for some pet cats along with a hamster (yes, Harlan the hamster has a very nice ring to it).

Hawk- is the last name of Packers linebacker, A.J. Hawk. A.J was the Packers first round draft pick in 2006 and was a reliable starter for 8 years. He was a major part of the super bowl XLV and while in college was one of the greatest linebackers to ever play for Ohio State.

Hawk would be a good name for any small pet bird, just for the irony of the name and also because it would be named after a solid football player too.

Holmgren- is the last name of coach Mike Holmgren. According to the Packers hall of fame, Holmgren accomplished what five head coaches before him had failed to do: He returned the Packers to prominence. Not since Vince Lombardi stepped down after winning his third straight NFL championship in 1967 had a

Packers coach departed Green Bay with a winning record. But over Holmgren's seven seasons, he led them to their first Super Bowl title in 29 years; compiled a .670 winning percentage in the regular-season, a figure topped only by Lombardi; and finished on the plus side of .500 every year, something the Packers had done only four times over their previous 24 years.

Holmgren would be a great name for a Saint Bernard since let's face it coach kind of looked like one. It would also be a good name for any pet that looks like it has a bad ass mustache like most breads of terriers.

Gilbert - is the first name of one of Packers fan favorites, Gilbert Brown. Gilbert was the big man in the middle of the Packers defense who was great at stopping the run. He was known for his big heart and big stomach. In fact he ate so much burger king that they named a burger for him.

Gilbert would be an amazing name for any dog or cat. Though Gilbert Brown was a large man, pets of all shapes and sizes can have this name. Gilbert for some reason is just a darn good per name.

Jacke- is the last name of Packers long time kicker, Chris Jacke. Chris was an all-pro in 1993 and a member of the Green Bay Packers hall of fame. He is also one of the top scorers in Packer history.

Jacke would be a good name for a breed of cat like a Chantilly-Tiffany or any kind of pet with a good head of hair. Chis Jacke had the best hair in the 1990's period!

Jennings- is the last name of Packers wide receiver, Greg Jennings. Greg is a two time pro-bowler and a super bowl champion. He was one of Brett Favre's favorite receivers later in his career.

Jennings would be a fine name for a sporty dog like a Vizsla or black lab or of course a golden retriever.

Jervey- is the last name of running back, Travis Jervey. Travis Jervey was the first Packer to make the pro-bowl as a special team player. He was also known for his free spirit and love for surfing which in some cases he may have loved more than football.

Jervey would be a great name for a pet lion. Fun fact: Travis Jervey had a pet lion named Nala . If you prefer a smaller feline then lion any cat would be honored to be named after this speedy Packer.

Kampman – is the last name of long time defensive end, Aaron Kampman. Aaron was one of the best Packer on the defense side of the ball from 2002 to 2009. During that time Kampman amassed 58 sacks and was a two time pro-bowler.

Kampman would be an amazing name for a pet kangaroo. It would also have a nice ring for most felines. "Come here Kampman the cat, time to watch the bears lose again".

McGarrahan- is the last name of Scott McGarrahan. Scott was a safety for the Green Bay Packers from 1998 to 2000 and contributed to the great super bowl 31 defense.

McGarrahan would be a noble name for an Irish setter or maybe Irish wolfhound. Heck any animal from the Emerald Isle would love the name McGarrahan.

McKenzie- is the last time of Packers long time Corner back, Mike McKenzie. Mike was a third round draft pick by the Packers in 1999 and became the starter in the Defensive backfield for the next ten years.

McKenzie would be a nice name for a smaller bread of cat or maybe going with the alliteration theme again go with McKenzie the Macaw

McMahon – is the last name of one time backup quarterback Jim McMahon. Yes, Jim Mcmahon was a Packer in 1995 and 1996 and even was part of the super bowl 31 team.

McMahon would be a good name for a pet that enjoys wearing sunglasses and has a low IQ. So basically if you're a true Packer fan and a pet owner this name should be low on the list.

Najeh – Is the first name of former Packer running back Najeh Davenport. Najeh was a third down back and a great compliment to Ahman Green in the Packers backfield during the early 2000s.

Najeh would be a nice name for a dog, cat, reptile, bird. It is a very nice pet name and should not be avoided just because of the rep he got from his actions in college. If you don't know what I'm talking about trust me you are lucky.

Navies- is the last name of former packer linebacker, Hannibal Navies. Hannibal was a steady linebacker and special team's player for the pack from 2003 to 2004.

Navies would be an awesome name for a pet turtle or snake. This name would also be great for a fish and maybe a very special dog or cat.

Paris- is the first name of former Packer Linebacker, Paris Lenon. Paris was a Packer from 2001- 2005 and played a major role both on defense but also on special teams.

Paris would be a great name for a Poodle . That's about it.

Pederson – is the last name of long time back-up quarterback, Doug Pederson. Doug was the back up to the great Brett Favre from 1995-1998 and then again from 2001- 2004. During his time in Green Bay Pederson was also the holder on field goals.

Pederson would be a great name for a Persian cat or maybe a Pekingese dog.

Reggie-is the first name of Packers legend Reggie White. Reggie was one of the greatest football players ever. During his career he was a two-time NFL Defensive Player of the Year, 13-time Pro Bowl, and 13-time All-Pro selection holds second place all-time among career sack leaders with 198 (behind Bruce Smith's 200 career sacks) and was selected to the NFL 75th Anniversary All-Time Team, NFL 1990s All-Decade Team, and the NFL 1980s All-Decade Team.

Reggie would be an amazing name for any pet. This is one of those names that is both a great legendary pet and Packer name so go with it.

Rison – is the last name of Wide Receiver, Andre Rison. Andre had a very brief Green Bay Packer career but will always be remembered for his big catch in Super Bowl 31.

Rison would be a nice baby name for a dog any type that likes to howl at the bad moon rison. Also again could be used for a golden retriever (I know been using that line for like every wide receiver)

Rivera- is the last name of Packers all-star guard Marco Rivera. Marco Played for Green Bay from 1996 to 2004. During that time, Marco was a 3 time pro bowler, super bowl champ and in 2011 was voted into the Packers Hall of Fame.

Rivera would be a great name for a vast number of pets. I could see it for any reptile, fish and some dogs.

Samkon- is the first name of former Green Bay Packers running back, Samkon Gado. Though only a packer for a very short time (2005-2006) his name still has a place in the hearts of many fans. Samkon was undrafted out of Liberty college and came to the Packers in a pinch when there were no running backs healthy to play.

Samkon would be an amazing name for a Samoyed dog or

maybe a Siberian Husky. For some reason this name only works for dogs and not cats.

Sterling- is the first name of Packer great Sterling Sharpe. Sterling Sharpe was one of the greatest wide receivers in Packer history and if it wasn't for an injury that cut his career short he would have been one of the NFL's all-time greats. During his short career Sharpe was a 5 time pro bowler and led the league in receptions 3 times.

Sterling would be a nice name for most pets. It really is universal but again for the 50th time in this book it would be great for a golden retriever.

Sydney- is the last name of Packers full back and former coach Harry Sydney. Harry is a three time super bowl champion and the only person to catch a touch down from all-time greats Brett Favre and Joe Montana.

Sydney would be an amazing pet name for both a dog and cat. I could see the name working for a Siberian husky or a Siamese cat.

Tauscher – is the last name of long time Packer offensive lineman, Mark Tauscher. Mark Is a hometown hero who grew up in Auburndale, Wisconsin, played football at UW Madison and then spend 10 years with the Packers

According to Brett Favre, Tauscher looked like at Pekingese so used his name for this dog breed or maybe any animal that is "fluffy" which a nice way to say fat.

Winters- is the last name of Packers long time center, Frank Winters. Frank was a pro bowl player and is in the Green Bay Packer hall of fame. He, along with Brett Favre and Mark Chmura were known as the three Packerinos.

Winters would be an amazing name for a dog that loves cold

weather and the snow. So if you have a sled dog name it Winters. The name will also work for a cat as well maybe one that is as white as snow.

Wolf- is the last name of NFL hall of fame, General Manager, Ron Wolf. Ron Wolf is widely credited with bringing success to a Packers franchise that had rarely won during the two decades prior. Some of Ron Wolf's greatest accomplishments are trading for a young Brett Favre and bring in one of the all-time great free agents to the Packers. During Ron Wolf's career he has been involved in Winning three super bowls.

Wolf would be a great name for a dog it could be for a breed like Shiloh Shepherd or Tamaskan which looks like one. The name could also be used to be ironic and used with a tiny little ankle bitter.

Aaron Rodgers era names

After backing up Brett Favre for the first three years of his NFL career, Rodgers became the Packers' starting quarterback in 2008 and has been one of the NFL's premier quarterbacks for last 12 years. The Highlight of this era has been the victory in Super Bowl XLV over the Pittsburgh Steelers. Also during the Rodgers era the Packers went to the Playoff's nine or the lasr13 years. This era has produced a lot of Winning football and a immense number of great players with amazing names. If you are looking for a modern name of a Champion take a gander of the list below:

Best names from this era:

Aaron Rodgers – is the first and last name of one of the Packers all–time great quarterbacks. Aaron Rodgers is known by many as the most talented quarterback in the NFL. He is a three time league most valuable player awards and an seven time Pro bowler. Rodgers currently has the NFL's all-time regular season career passer rating record and is one of two quarterbacks to have a regular season career passer rating of over 100, the other being Russell Wilson. Rodgers is fifth all-time in postseason career passer rating, has the best touchdown-to-interception ratio in NFL history at 4.23, holds the league's lowest career interception percentage at 1.5 percent and the highest single-season passer rating record of 122.5. Due to the fact that Rodgers is the NFL's all-time regular season career passer rating leader, and his overall high level of play, Rodgers is considered by some sportscasters and players to be one of the greatest quarterbacks of all time

Aaron Rodgers is a great name for any and every pet owned by a Packers fan. This is one of the all-time great names and should be used for an all-time great pet.

Blake- is the first name of middle linebacker, Blake Martinez. Blake has been a tackling machine since entering the NFL in

2016. Martinez in 2017 had 144 tackles which was the most in the league, he was also a pro-bowl alternate the last two seasons.

Blake would be an awesome name for a bull dog or most tough breeds of dogs. I'm not a fan of the name for cats but maybe a gerbil or hamster.

Bulaga – is the last name of Offensive Lineman, Bryan Bulaga. Bryan, when healthy is one of the better offensive tackles in the game. He was also the youngest person to start in a super

This name is perfect for your pet whale or maybe something smaller like your gold fish. This name could be used for larger breeds of dogs as well.

Driver- is the last name of one of the all-time great receivers, Donald Driver. Donald holds the all-time packer receiving record for most 1,000 yard seasons, most receiving yards in a career, and most consecutive games with a reception. Not to mention Driver is a super bowl Champion and a Packer hall of famer.

Driver would be an amazing name for any athletic pet that loves to run and jump. And for the 51st time in this book I would recommend it would recommend it for a golden retriever.

Chillar – is the last name of former linebacker, Brandon Chillar. Brandon was great at tackling, forcing fumbles and also was an instrumental part of the Packers Super bowl championship defense. Today Packer fans can find Brandon Chillar as one of the chief investors in the Elite Football league of India.

Chillar would be a nice name for a chinchilla or a chow chow. Basically any pet that starts with a "C". Chillar the cat, sound pretty sweet too.

Clay – is the first name of Packer great, Clay Mathews. Clay is a six time pro bowler and the Defensive player of year in 2010.

Clay Mathews is known for having a "motor that never stops" and is great at getting the big sack when it matters most.

Clay would be a remarkable name for a cat or a fish but not so much for a dog. Though Clay Mathews was a "bad ass" on the field, the name seems to be kind of unexciting for a pet.

Collins- is the last name of Packers safety, Nick Collins. Nick was one of the best defense backs in Packer history . During his amazing career that was cut short by a neck injury, he was a three time pro bowler, NFL interception leader and Super Bowl champion.

Collins would be a great name for a Collie or again a Cat, I think I'm getting lazy so just going with the alliteration thing again.

Equanimeous – is the first name of the Packers often hurt wide receiver Equanimeous St. Brown. He did not see the field much but does have an interesting name.

This name would good for a fish, or reptile. Basically any pet that you do not need to call on a regular basis. It also sounds like a very appropriate name for a horse.

Finely- is the last name of Packers pro-bowl tight end, Jermichale Finely. Jermichale was a Packer from 2008 to 2013 before a neck injury ended his career. During his short playing career, Finely was one of the best pass catching tight ends in the game.

Finely is a no brainer name for a pet Fish. MIC DROP!

Geronimo- is the first name of up and coming wide receiver Geronimo Allison. Geronimo was developing into one of Aaron Rodgers favorite targets before injury cut his season short.

Geronimo will be a decent name for a German Shepard or a Gerbil. It's a fun name so think about using it if you have a unique pet.

Grant – is the last name of Packers running back, Ryan Grant. Ryan Grant was a pro-bowl running back and Super bowl champion. He is best known by Packers fans for a huge playoff game against Seattle where he rushed for 206 yards and 3 touchdowns.

Grant would be a nice name for a beagle or any nice loyal pet.

Hayward – is the last name of defensive back, Casey Hayward. Casey was a second round draft pick of the Packers in 2012 and ever since stepping foot on a NFL field has been able to be a ball-hawk / turn over machine. Hayward let the NFL in interceptions in 2016 and is a two time pro-bowler.

Hayward would be a great name for a Husky or a Himalayan cat. This name works with cats, dogs and even some birds.

Jackson – is the last name of packers 3rd down back, Brandon Jackson. Brandon was a dependable back-up to Ryan Grant and James Stark. He was also a key member to the Super Bowl 45 championship team.

Jackson would be an amazing name for a most pets. Try it with your Javanese cat or your Jack Russel Terrier. Or you can name you first born Jackson but that is for another book.

James Jones – is the first and last name of one of the most popular packers in the Aaron Rodgers era. Jones led the NFL in touchdowns in 2012 and was a big part of some of the most explosive offenses in league history.

James Jones would be a great name for an athletic cat that likes to jump around. It is also a fun name for a bird.

Jordy- is the first name of one of the most loved player in Packer in history, Jordy Nelson. Jordy was also one of the best receivers in Packer history and for many years was one of the best "deep ball" threats in football. One could argue that Nelson was Aaron

Rodgers favorite target and his 72 touchdown total could justify that.

Jordy would be an amazing name for a Golden Retriever. Yes I went there again but it will be the last time. Jordy is one of those name that is pretty universal for any pet and would be highly approved by any Packer fan.

Kapri – is the first name of little known running back Kapri Bibbs, Kapri came to the Packers midseason in 2018 and has been a third string running back who only saw the field from the sidelines for most of the year. The good news is he has a really great name.

Kapri would be a great name for a bird or a fish but only the most hardcore Packer fan would know who the heck your pet was named after.

Kingsley – is the first name of Packers D-lineman Kingsley Keke. Kingsley has yet to play a snap during the writing of this book. He is a was promising rookie and has a great name but he found himself in the dog house (no pun intended) and then cut from the team.

Kingsley would be a nice name for a cockatoo. It also sounds nice for most dogs and cats. Kingsley is overall a great pet name but not the most legendary Packer name so keep that in consideration.

Kumerow- is the last name of Packers fan favorite receive, Jake Kumerow. Jake was a UW- Whitewater legend and what little time he has had with the Packers did not disappoint.

Kumerow would be an amazing name for any and all pets. As a Packer fan who lives in Wisconsin this name is a Win / Win. It is also rumored that Aaron Rodgers has a pet dog named Kumerow.

Lattimore – is the last name of Linebacker, Jamari Lattimore. Jamari was a steady force on both special team and rushing the quarterback during 2011-2014 season.

Lattimore would be a nice name for a tough breed of dog like Pitbull or Doberman. I could see it work for a turtle and some fish as well.

Linsley- is the last name of Packers center, Corey Linsley. Corey has been one of the most consistent offensive lineman in the NFL since being drafted in 2014. Linsley is known for his quick feet and ability to read the defense and call out switches to his fellow O-lineman.

Linsley would be a good for a Lykoi cat or maybe a bird. Linsley may also work for some smaller dogs and fluffy cats.

Lumpkin- is the last name of Packers back up running back Kregg Lumpkin. Kregg played two years for the Packers and was really only known because his named rhymes with pumpkin.

Lumpkin will be a great name of only a specific cat breed, a Lambkin. It could be a cute name for a turtle or a fish as well.

Marcedes – is the first name of veteran tight end Marcedes Lewis. Marcedes has been a Packer at the tail end of his career and does not see much playing time, However in his prime he was one of the best tight ends in football and was a pro- bowler in 2010.

Marcedes is a great pet and football player name. This is one of those names that could be used for any and all breeds and types of fur babies you may have.

Mason – is the first name of Packers all-time scoring leader, Mason Crosby. Mason has been the Packers kicker since 2007 and during that time has been one of the best in the NFL. Mason is a Super bowl champion and future Packer hall of famer.

Mason would be an awesome name for any loyal dependable pet. I picture a black lab that lays next you on the couch well watching the game or a cat that comes to the door to comfort you after a playoff loss.

Starks- is the last name of running back James Starks. James was a 6th round draft by the Packers in 2010. As a rookie James contributed greatly to winning Super Bowl 45 and holds a number of rookie playoff rushing records for his performance that year. In the years after the Super Bowl Starks was a powerful rusher with great hands out of the backfield.

Starks would be as great name for a Siamese cat or any other feline breed that start with an "S". I also like this name for any pet bird you may have.

Woodson – is the last name of Packers all-time great, Charles Woodson. Charles was a 9 time pro-bowler along with being named defensive player of the year in 2009. Woodson is a member of the NFL 2000's all-decade team and is soon to be in both The Packers and pro football hall of fames.

Woodson would be an amazing name for any pet. He is an iconic Packer and person, so use this name! The name like the person has a lot of swagger and oozes out coolness.

Final Thought's

Pet owners have the duty to give their new fur baby a good name, (hopefully a Packer name), however your job as a pet owner does not end when it's new printed on its tags. In Fact, the act of being a pet owner never ends and should be a very important and rewarding part of your life regardless of your pet's name.

Remember overall a pet's name doesn't matter, what does is that your new pet, get genuine, unconditional love.

Bibliography

"Birth of a Team and a Legend". Green Bay Packers. Archived from *the original* on February 18, 2014. Retrieved December 12, 2016.

^ *"Club Information"* (PDF). 2019 Green Bay Packers Media Guide. NFL Enterprises, LLC. July 30, 2019. Retrieved September 4, 2019.

^ *"Green Bay Packers Team Capsule"* (PDF). 2018 Official National Football League Record and Fact Book. NFL Enterprises, LLC. August 9, 2018. Retrieved August 14, 2018.

^ Jump up to:[a] [b] *"Shareholders"*. Packers.com. NFL Enterprises, LLC. Retrieved January 22, 2015.

^ *"Birth of a Team, and a Legend"* (PDF). 2018 Green Bay Packers Media Guide. NFL Enterprises, LLC. September 12, 2018. Retrieved May 8, 2019.

^ Jump up to:[a] [b] Names, Larry D (1987). "The Myth". In Scott, Greg (ed.). The History of the Green Bay Packers: The Lambeau Years. *1*. Angel Press of WI. p. 30. *ISBN* *0-939995-00-X*.

^ *"Chronology of Professional Football"* (PDF). National Football League. January 22, 2015. Retrieved January 22, 2015.

^ *"Green Bay Packers Team History"*. Pro Football Hall of Fame. Retrieved February 24, 2016.

^ Jump up to:[a] [b] *Zirin, Dave (January 25, 2011). "Those Non-Profit Packers". The New Yorker.* Retrieved December 28, 2014.

^ Jump up to:[a] [b] *"Super Bowls & Championships"*. Green Bay Packers. Retrieved December 12, 2016.

^ {{cite web|url=https://www.pro-football-reference.com/teams/gnb/

^ *"The Acme Packers were short-lived"*. packers.com. Retrieved August 1, 2018.

^ *"A name 90 years in the making"*. archive.jsonline.com. Retrieved August 1, 2018.

^ *"The truth and myth about 'The Hungry Five'"*. packers.com. Retrieved August 1, 2018.

^ *"Dec. 8, 1929: Packers earn first league title"*. Retrieved August 1, 2018.

^ *"History of Champions: Packers are No. 1 in NFL"*. Press Gazette Media. Retrieved August 1, 2018.

^ *"Team Records: Games Won"* (PDF). National Football League. Retrieved December 12, 2016.

^ *"Don Hutson: Information from"*. Answers.com. Retrieved February 7, 2011.

^ Fleming, David (September 27, 2013). *"Blaze of Glory"*. *ESPN*. Retrieved December 9, 2014.

^ Maraniss, David (September 14, 1999). *"In throes of winter, a team in disarry is reborn"*. *Milwaukee Journal Sentinel*. Milwaukee, Wisconsin. p. 2B. Retrieved July 6, 2011.

^ Pennington, Bill (January 16, 2008). *"NYTimes article of January 15, 2008"*. The New York Times. Retrieved February 7, 2011.

^ *"Vince Lombardi Record, Statistics, and Category Ranks | Pro-Football-Reference.com"*. Pro-Football-Reference.com. Retrieved August 1, 2018.

^ *"AP Was There: 1967 Cowboys-Packers Ice Bowl game"*. USA Today. Retrieved August 1, 2018.

^ *"The 100 Greatest Moments in Sports History | The Ice Bowl"*. Sports Illustrated's 100 Greatest Moments. Retrieved August 1, 2018.

^ Old School Packers Archived February 18, 2006, at the Wayback Machine from the Milwaukee Journal Sentinel website. Retrieved February 5, 2007

About the Author

Dr. Jon Kester was born in Wisconsin Rapids in 1979, though not named after any Packers he right out of the whom was a fan of all sports in the Great State of Wisconsin. This included at the time a not so great Green Bay Packers teams of the 1980s. Dr. Kester recalls as a boy being made fun of for wearing a Packer jacket on the school bus. Lucky for Jon Kester the 80s ended sooner than later and soon the whole bus was wearing Packer clothing. During the 1990s Dr. Kester started a his now massive collection of Green Bay Packer memorabilia. This includes rare one of a kind items like, a Curley Lambeau autographed photo and Donald Driver's neon sign from his TV show. As an adult, Kester formed a great love and aspiration for the Packers amazing history and did everything he could to learn about the players and coaches that made the team great. After getting a master's degree in sports administration Dr. Kester had only one place he wanted to work and that was Lambeau Field, he was lucky to get hired in 2008.

During his 15 plus years of living and working in Green Bay,Jon has met many people named after Packer players. In fact a baby named Aaron Rodgers is what inspired him to write this book. Kester does not only have a love for the Packers but also babies more specifically his own three babies which he may or may not name after Packer players. Besides the Green Bay Packers and Kids Dr. Kester also has a love for writing and has published five other books. Kester is constantly working on his next great book so more will be coming soon!

Printed in the United States
by Baker & Taylor Publisher Services